Money can't buy happiness

This book belongs to

_____

Written by Stephen Barnett
Illustrated by Rosie Brooks

Contents

About this book

A well-crafted book with two stories based on social values which will help the young learners to enhance their reading skills. Colourful illustrations add to its charm.

Money can't buy happiness

'I'd really like to be rich,' my brother said to me. It was raining and we were inside playing board games. It would be fun to be able to buy anything I wanted!'
'But I don't think it would make you very happy if you weren't happy already,' I said.

4

Mum was sitting nearby and reading. When she heard what we were talking about she said, 'I think that this is true. Having enough money for our needs helps us to be happy. But more money than you need, won't make you any happier.'

'But just think about all of the great things you could do with a lot of money,' said my brother, excitedly. For example, I could . . .

. . . buy a big red sports car ...

. . . go to movies every night . . .

. . . eat ice cream every day.'

'But often, the people who spend their lives chasing money aren't the happiest. They are always busy buying different things. But they are not always happy as we think,' said mother. 'Look at Mr. Black who's always busy buying and selling things. But have you ever seen him smiling?'

I thought about this for a moment. Mum was right. Sometimes spending the extra money can become a difficult task.

'Money is necessary of course,' Mum continued, 'and it's good to have some extra money at times. But many people put too much value on chasing money.'

'And it's not good to always buy new things to replace the old. This makes people dissatisfied with their lives. The trouble comes when people value everything only in terms of money! You only need money for what you want to buy, not for what you might want in future.'

'It is far better to spend any extra time you have on doing things that will make you happy rather than to spend it on buying things,' continued mother.

14

'In the end one has to think about what one needs, not what one wants. And one should count the blessings for the things one already has.'

'Even if I had all the money in the world I wouldn't be any happier than with what I have now!'

I have learnt this

I was on a visit to my great aunt on a weekend. We were in her kitchen having lunch when she said, 'Do you know, when you get to my age, it's a funny thing that life becomes very clear about what is important and what is not.'

'When you're younger you become too busy with life and the things you're doing to think much about it. But towards the end of your life, you learn that there are only a handful of things that really matter.'
'What are those?' I asked, curiously.

'First,' my great aunt said, 'is not to judge people too quickly. Wait until you know the situation and all the facts before you decide to judge someone.'

'Your friends and family are the most important things in the world. Nothing can take their place!'

'Responsibility is another very important aspect. You must always take the responsibility for anything you do.'

'Treat people as you would like to be treated by others.'

'Forgive. We all need at times to be forgiven for the things we've done. And we need to forgive others for the things that they have done.'

'Remember that tomorrow is another day.
Sometimes when things are difficult it is best to
stop, get some rest and then start again the
next day.'

'Time heals everything. The things that we think we will never get over, stops troubling us after a while.'

'Accept failure as well as success. Enjoy when you succeed at something, and understand that sometimes you will also fail at some things. Accept that as well.'

'Believe in yourself that you can achieve everything under the sun provided you have the determination.'

'Listen to others. Be respectful when people speak. Listen patiently to what they have to say.'

'And that's all you need to remember to have a good, successful and satisfied life,' my great aunt said.

New words

board

raining

rich

happier

excitedly

chasing

buying

happiest

spend

different

extra

different

difficult

continued

necessary

value

dissatisfied

terms

replace

trouble

future

blessings

already

count

think

funny

important

towards

handful

curiously

learnt

busy

judge

decide

responsibility

treated

forgiven

tomorrow

hurts

success

understand

fail

believe

determination

achieve

patiently

remember

satisfied

What did you learn?

Money can't buy happiness
What were the brothers playing?
What was the name of their neighbour?
What did the mother say that people should count?

I have learnt this
Whom was the girl visiting?
What were the things that great aunt said
were important?
What was the colour of great aunt's clothes?